D1366752

The Unfurling

Nimah Ismail Nawwab

Selwa Press
P.O. Box 3650
Vista, California 92085 U.S.A.

Publisher's Cataloging-in-Publication
(Provided by Quality Books, Inc.)

Nawwab, Nimah Ismail.
    The unfurling/Nimah Ismail Nawwab
    p.cm
    LCCN: 2004111863
    ISBN: 0-9701157-9-2

    1. Middle East--History--Poetry. 2. Women--Saudi
Arabia--Poetry. 3. Saudi Arabia--Poetry. I. Title.

PS3614.A9334U64 2004   811'.6
                           QB104-800010

        9 8 7 6 5 4 3 2 1

    Printed in the United States of America

    Cover and illustrations by Karim Ramis
    Copyright © Karim Ramis 2004

iv

The poet should seize the Particular, and ... thus represent the Universal.

Johann Wolfgang von Goethe, quoted in Johann Peter Eckermann's Conversations with Goethe, June 11, 1825

Poems

Awakenings

Contours

Crossroads

To a cheering squad of family and friends without whose support this book would have never been completed.

Foreword

From the heart of Arabia – perhaps from the very soul of the Saudi Arabs – come the evocative contents of this remarkable book of poetry. The gift of author Nimah Ismail Nawwab is to capture the flavor, indeed, the aroma, of old and new Arabia and waft it enchantingly before us like frankincense or myrrh.

So compelling is this poetic sensation that we are drawn into captivating imagery that mysteriously transports us across the burning sands of time. It's a magical journey replete with delightful rewards of vibrant, lifelike vistas – so absorbing we may feel ourselves making the crossing!

Yet the book is far more than an expedition into the past, no matter the tantalizing discoveries. It also is a voyage of self-discovery and revelation into the world of woman. Layers of culture pass before our eyes as we navigate realms of deep feeling, emotion, suffering, courage, love and hope. In reality, powerful words carry us beyond women to embrace all humanity. Herein, the real exploration is into the wonders of the rich and complex human tableau.

We may marvel, admire, stand in awe; we also may stagger, gape or feel overwhelmed. These common threads, and others, bind humanity in time and space, forever. The essence of the human experience, of family, friends, and faith, resonate at the core, weaving an indelible path across the pages of this book.

Nimah also confronts today's dynamic world by looking beyond Arabia to share her own restless energy, courage and – above all – optimism for the future. Always, she writes with a poignancy, compassion and relevance that touches the mind and heart. Her journey is our journey. It is one to be treasured!

*Michael Skinner, author of **Grandeur in the Stars** a book of free verse poetry, is a longtime journalist. He strongly believes poetic words and images can penetrate into the human soul and help guide humanity toward global peace and social justice.*

Acknowledgements

I would like to thank the following for their inspiration, enthusiasm, encouragement and invaluable assistance.

My family supported me emotionally on many levels, bore with my late hours and patiently listened to repeated readings. To the most supportive cheering squad one could have, I am truly grateful.

There are numerous poets, writers, teachers, and friends from various parts of the world to whom I owe a debt that I can never repay. Starting off with the global team of contributing editors including my scholarly father Ismail Ibrahim Nawwab who read Shakespeare to me at the age of eight; the peace activist, culturally knowledgeable Michael Skinner; Aisha Kay for her enthusiasm, discerning sharp eyes and support at all hours day and night and Sheree Mack for her direct approach to poems.

Karim Ramis for his illustrations and creativity; 'my inspiration' Naomi Shihab Nye; Nathalie Handal for my 'first knocks;' Audrey Shabbas, John Duke Anthony, John Esposito and Mohja Kahf for contributing to the reviews despite their extremely busy schedules; poetry companions Deirdre Tyler and Anne Norberg; DD for challenging me to persevere and finish this venture; and Vicci Thompson for her invaluable and continued support through her website at www.aramcoexpats.com.

Steve Seager, Tamara Myatt, Marian Bukhari, writers Paul Lunde, Bill Tracy, Bob Norberg, Mary Norton; The Arabian Reading Association (TARA) Conference Committee Chairperson, Anna Marie Amudi; Robert Arndt editor of *Saudi Aramco World* magazine; poet Antwian Crawford; Emad Dughaither, Carolyn Thomas, Debra Nuaimi; Phil Embleton for finally joining in the poetic foray and numerous others who are too modest to want their names to appear in print; they know who they are and how grateful I am to them.

I also wish to extend my sincere thanks and gratitude to a special person, my publisher Tim Barger who embraced this book project with enthusiasm and whose advice, work and long hours kept us both going, bridging time zones and countries.

My gratitude also to the students and readers who have corresponded with me and inspired me to continue writing.

Nimah Ismail Nawwab

Awakenings

The Longing

Freedom,
How her spirit
Haunts,
Hooks,
Entices us all!

Freedom,
Will the time come
For my ideas to roam
Across this vast land's deserts,
Through the caverns of the Empty Quarter?

For my voice to be sent forth,
Crying out in the stillness of a quiet people,
A voice among the voiceless?

For my thoughts, that hurl around
In a never-ending spiral,
To settle
To mature, grow and flourish
In a barren wasteland of shackled minds?

Will my spirit be set free—
To soar above the undulating palm fronds?
Will my essence and heart be unfettered,
Forever
Freed,
Of man-made Thou Shall Nots?

Gentleness Stirred

Striding through the gates of learning,
Wrapped warmly in her black *abaya*,
Modestly cloaked head to toe,
Not a hair astray, nor skin showing,
Holding her head up high,
Thinking of the future,
Arms laden with books,
Head in the clouds,
Lunch, television, studies, friends,
That is how her day will go
Near future, far future,
Blissful, brimming with expectations.

"Hey, you there!" thunders across the parking lot
"You with the black boots" the tone is raised
Oh, oh, reluctantly she turns,
Fear stirs,
Flinching,
Watches wrath unleashed.

The self-righteous, bushy-bearded figure,
Crashes through the crowds,
Bestriding his narrow world like a Colossus,
As his entourage hurries in his wake,
A raging bull on the rampage,
Seeing red as the girl flouts 'convention.'
Necks crane to watch,
The crowds are in on the show.
He thunders on,
The police by his side

"Stop, your scarf has slipped."
The tirade begins, gains momentum.

Head cast down,
Eyes to the ground,
Shoulders drooping
She listens,
Afraid,
Confused,
Cringing,
Burrowing into her deepest self.

Has she missed a prayer?
Has she been a disobedient daughter?
Cheated, lied, stolen,
Beaten a child, an animal, been cruel to another soul?

What did she do?
Her scarf slipped,
An unforgivable transgression,
In the eyes of the Controllers.
Is that her sin,
Her ever-lasting humiliation,
Her major fall from grace,
Her offense?

The mind is strange, the spirit stranger yet,
The rebellion begins.

** Abaya is the outer garment worn by women in Arabian gulf
countries.*

The Hidden Layers

Some think I am hiding
Underneath my long black cloak,
With little narrow slits for my eyes,
Cloaked in mystery, medieval modesty,
Wondering, what is going on behind the mask?

Comfortable with their own tunnel vision,
Construing their own scenarios,
Little knowing that I am proud,
Proud of my identity,
Proud of my femininity,
Proud of my spirit,
My faith,
My mind, not just my body,
Proud of my heritage, culture, long-entrenched traditions.

But modest in my dress,
Modest in my demeanor,
Modest in my expectations,
Viewing the world with sharp eyes,
Viewing all with curiosity and a thirst to learn.

Does my cloak, my masked visage,
Long viewed by outsiders with pity,
Barricade me from the world?
Or does it open up vistas of wonder,
Open up doors for exploration into the unseen,
Open up the world through a different hidden sharp lens?

My world is my oyster, as it is for my unveiled sisters.
Their choices are made as are mine.
I remain cloaked, they remain uncloaked.
All united by unbreakable bonds of sisterhood.

Fiery Embrace

Small slender wisps unfurl,
Flames flicker,
Fire soon follows,
The blaze spreads,
Fiery deluge feeds, consumes, devours,
Time and fire, fire and time
Speed on, and on and on…

Wails arise with the breaking news,
Denial,
Shock,
Immobility,
Panic,
Slow movement,
Jerky, hasty movement,
The stampede begins.

Girls screaming,
Teachers shouting,
Frenzy reigns,
Classes running amok,
In the Holy City's school.

Corridors fill up, stairways too,
Tempestuous fire surges, girls surge on,
The race is lost,
Pile ups begin,
Bodies jamming,
Colliding,
Toppling over,
Falling,
Running figures tread over the fallen.

Awakenings

The lucky first racing onto the street,
Crying out for help,
Crying in relief,
Assistance arrives,
Finally, oh deliverance at last.

Shouts ring out enflamed with rage,
"No, go back, go back, your *abaya*s,
How can you leave uncovered,
Unshielded from male eyes?"
Fanatical figures shove them back,
Back into the inferno,
Back to burning halls of learning.

"Your *abayas,*
Cover up,
How dare you?
Go back," they bellow
Rough hands,
Dark visages,
Raised voices do their work,
Relentless in their self-appointed, protective mission.

Cowering young girls,
Dragging their feet,
Retreat,
To the grisly scene.
Gazes turn inward bid farewell to hope,
One last outward, backward glance,
Bidding farewell to the clean air, busy street,
Bidding farewell to their family, future
Bidding farewell to their very lives.

Appointment with Life

The phone rings,
A dispassionate voice on the phone,
Non committal:
"Results suspicious;
Need clarification.
The doctor wants another scan."

Dread sets in,
Coldness creeps across,
Mind benumbed,
Fear,
Trepidation,
Silent despair takes hold.

Slowly the decision is made.
Disregard,
Forget,
Brush the notion aside.

Live and wait,
Time slows, drags.
Till the moment comes for a yes or a no,
For a life-changing prognosis.

Alone in countless ways,
Deep thoughts prevail,
Mind still closed up,
Thoughts run on unchecked.
Chemicals,
Radiation,

Body waging a war
Devouring cells, nerves, stamina
The dreaded word with a capital C
Is contemplated.
Years to live or to be cut short.
Friends and family,
How will they deal with the news?

An appointment is set up,
Standing patiently,
Hospital gown untied,
The intimidating machines are set up.
Oh what cold, cold machines,
Cold feelings, cold room,
Coldness closes in.

Pain sets in momentarily,
The machine lets up,
Tight grip eases,
Setting free as tests are done.

Black film against the lighted screen,
Embodying a reality,
White spots here and there,
Mysterious,
Frightening,
Worrisome.
Doctor arrives,
Scans,
Contemplates,
Pronounces judgment.

The Reprieve

Doctor looks straight into the eyes,
Gently, soothingly conveys the news,
Prognosis clear, news good,
A sigh of relief, a taxing burden lifted,
The looming shadow
Of things coming to a close,
Disappearing.

Life to be celebrated,
Each moment a treasure,
To be lived to the fullest,
Hope rises,
Resolutions are made.

Pleasures long forgotten,
Unappreciated,
Come back in full force,
Sights, scents, sounds amplified,
Major moments of life,
Of birth,
Of forming bonds,
Of closeness,
Of laughter,
Of joy shared,
Of the coming of minds,
Of simple smiles exchanged,
Of spiritual ecstasy,
Of the good and bad,
Of pleasures and tribulations
Savored in full.
Treasures beyond compare.

Shrouded Mystery

Shrouded, cloaked in black,
Figures of mystery,
Tales abound of their lives,
True or false, that is the question.
What does one do
With masked figures
While looking deep into the hidden folds?

Trying to decipher the looks in the black fringed eyes,
The lives they lead,
Choices they make,
Are their lives as secluded as they appear?

Or are they full of personal successes,
Of strong family ties,
Unbreakable friendships,
Of an unshakeable faith?

Life Imprisonment

The world has darkened in her eyes
She is left reeling,
Crushed,
Shattered,
Shackled,
Trapped in an iron-clad deadly web,
Attacked again and again by the vile tormenter,
Internal shrieks echo through her very being,
Endlessly.

Living in limbo,
Neither married nor divorced,
Murky, undefined state of being,
Former mate seizing all his powers of authority,
Payback time in effect,
As she is left hanging,
Hanging,
Hanging.

II

The engulfing darkness grows
Heavier,
Thicker.

Doors slammed in her face time and again,
Opportunities fizzling out,
Helplessly watching,
She turns about looking for a glimmer,
A small ray of light in the darkening world.
Hopes, drives, dreams

Loom out of reach,
A beckoning mirage.

Each intercession foiled,
Family, friends helplessly stand by,
"Oh the poor girl, what can be done"
A reverberating refrain,
Unable to escape stifling surroundings by traveling.
Thirst for knowledge, need for work unrealized,
As permission to travel, learn, work,
Remain in her keeper's hands,
For daring to leave a living nightmare,
His fury unappeased,
He withholds it all,
Money, recognition, her very identity.

A non entity.

III

Dark despair sets in,
Her constant companion.
Belittled by demonic dominance,
Battered,
Bleeding,
From open, untended wounds.
With each sluggish passing year,
Anguish intensifies.

Sinking deep into apathy,
She silently cries out,

The Unfurling

When will the merciless one
Find a drop of mercy,
The hands of justice release her,
From her invisible, invincible bonds,
To pursue her path?

The world has darkened.
A complete enshrouding darkness
Descends, seeps into her core.

Life itself hangs in the balance,
Her fate in jeopardy,
As she is left, hanging,
Hanging,
Hanging.

Better a wife to Henry the Eighth,
Than be buried alive.

The Indomitable Lady

*H*er soft silver locks shining,
The sun rays filter through the window,
Casting a large shadow on the wall,
Larger in shadow than life?

A life spent in tireless toil,
Married off young,
Bearing youngsters by the dozen,
Setting out banquets fit for a sultan,
Tutoring,
Wiping sick brows,
Worrying her life away.

Children quickly grown and married off,
Sleepless by the bedside of a sick husband,
Grieving over his abandonment from life,
Marrying off the rest without a partner,
She perseveres,
Holding on tightly to sanity, to patience,
As the world changes, time slows.

Beset by a frail body,
Pride holding her up,
Facing the troubles of nascent generations,
Of marriages gone wrong,
Of spoilt grandchildren,
Unmindful of the need
To let her enjoy a life of peace.

Her pampering will never be returned in full measure,
Her care-worn back, hand, forehead,

The Unfurling

Long years of suffering without a murmur,
She continues, till finally,
One notices that it is time to let her rest,
To pamper her and give her due,
Yet she gently turns them aside,
Unused to the attention, for once,
Shining on her and not on others.

The Beggar

The wizened face looks out onto the street
Her deep gaze full
Of a life-long struggle
To exist.

Dignity personified,
Banded head held high,
Peaceful in the rush of cars whizzing by,
Slowing down the pace for those who notice.

Her hands held out,
Graceful, rough hands,
Tiny, dark old-age spots proudly touted,
A badge of honor.

In a land of gushing black gold,
Of superhighways,
She stands on the edge of the fast lane
In need of sustenance.

Will passers-by stop, stare and forget,
Or think long and hard,
Of the possibility of a shared fate?

Winds of the Market

Stepping out of the shiny car,
Wrapped in black silk studded with glitter
Face uncovered, hair modestly covered
Turning onto the busy street,
Striding next to jean-clad teenaged girls
Showing off their latest fashionable cloaks
Shoppers in a hurry, barely looking at each other.

Clanking bracelets, crying babies
Swishing thobes and sliding *abayas*,
The sweet smell of waffle-like ice cream cones
Shawarmah cooking on the spit,
Pita bread brushed with *tahinah*, filled with mint leaves,
Roasted slivers topped with tomatoes, pickles
Corn on the cob dribbled with butter,
Served on sticks, wrapped in plastic,
Lined up youngsters
Awaiting popcorn, *shawarmah*, slush
Smells merging, wafting through the mall,
A hook.

Air-conditioned shops spotlighted in the mall
Indian cushions, Italian shoes
Swiss watches, Danish crystal
German garments, American gym shoes.
Every need catered for, every desire satiated.

Cold, stiff, formal, efficient,
The zing of the cashier drawers,
The swoosh of the credit card,
I am done.

II

My mother's realm of quaint shops,
Lantern lights falling onto fresh sweet meats,
Vendors balancing heavy bundles of Egyptian cotton,
Young boys strutting with trays of *halwa*,
Weaving through the crowd,
Shouting out the wares, their prices.

Graceful, quick hands
Pulling on the widening circles of dough,
Whirling the pastry discs in the air,
Stuffing them with meat, green onions,
Folding them into *mutabbaq* squares,
Each at their stalls,
Involved, busy, sweaty,
Strollers passing by, nodding to each other,
To the familiar and unfamiliar.

African ladies selling peanuts,
Measuring them out in blue tin cans,
Clicking against the sides of the container,
Soothing cradling strapped youngsters,
Beaming shopkeepers,
Softly inviting,
Hospitality a must.

Wares from the region,
Yemeni silver, Chinese brocade,
Syrian lamb wool cloaks,
Hand-made *Najdi* sandals, family-made *Hijazi iqals*,
Shown off with pride.

Haggling and bargaining
Taking up the time,
Carefully choosing, prudently selecting,
Paying in hard-earned coins,
As she leaves satisfied.

* *Mutabbaq,* a pastry prepared in Arabia and Yemen, means folded up.
** *Najdi* and *Hijazi* refer to the central and western regions of the Kingdom of Saudi Arabia.
*** *Iqal* is a head band often woven in black that holds a man's *ghutra* or headaddress in place.

The Step

*I*t all lies before her,
A window leading to the unknown,
A mirage that will solidify?

The day has come,
The life-turning decision,
Should she or shouldn't she,
Take that step?

Her upbringing has led to this moment,
Told throughout her life of her mission,
Of a goal that must be achieved,
Of a lifetime that must be embraced,
Contemplated by her, her mother, her family
As the ultimate of all ultimates.

Will she choose the life foreseen as complete,
Will she answer the call of duty,
The pervasive pull of tradition,
The enveloping need of womanhood,
Or will she turn her back, wait for another day,
Another choice?

Beginnings

Torn from my homeland,
Family on the run,
New land, new language,
Expectations arise.

Adjusting to the new life,
New sounds,
New faces,
New weather, new places,
New education,
New friends,
New beginnings or ends?

II

A new life has begun,
With all its temptations, pleasures,
All its challenges,
The identity evolving, shaping out,
Inner self remaining the same.

Balancing out, filtering out,
An alien to one place,
Yet an alien to the beloved homeland,
Needing the emotional bonds,
Language, scents of the homeland.

A big empty hole,
A constant ache,
Reminders of bygone time, land, family.

Balancing out, filtering out,
Coming onto its own,
At peace in its uniqueness.

Groves of Valor

*F*ronds lay stiff, unyielding,
The erect lines intimidating,
Silent sentinels in the quiet barren groves,
Bearing witness to centuries of endurance.

People joining in for short spans,
Young and old reaping the bounty,
Loyal fans and admirers of the fertile fronds,
Golden, red, and dark brown ambrosia
Savored by countless minions,
Their fame reaching the heights
As travelers pick up the thread of craving,
Carrying a token of the land and its people back home.

Fruitful years for the palm and people,
Expand, diminish and vanish,
Tales, histories unfold,
Told and untold,
Of the people and their sentinels,
Bearing witness to the drama of life.

Groves drying up, graves filling up,
Leaving behind traces in the sand
Ashes of burnt palms,
Ashes of dry bone,
Joining, mixing, forming yet another bond
Once again,
As destiny and fate rule.

The Ebb

I happen to be tired of being a man.
-Pablo Neruda

Surging through the seasons of life,
Body and mind,
Buffeted by the forces of change.

Endless hours at the office hooked to the PC,
Tested and tried,
Perpetual proving of expertise,
Office politics wreak their havoc.
Coming back to earth,
World politics pull and twist,
Binding us in dark bonds of despair.
No say in the winding ways of the murky world.

Visiting friends, sipping warm cappuccino,
Bonding, laughing, crying,
Homeward bound,
Time and again,
Searching for solitude,
Looking for time to assess the changes.

I am tired of being a woman,
With a woman's burdens,
Woman's ideals,
Navigating a world,
Where the shadows of women ebb and flow.

The Hand

I look at my hand,

A hand that has touched much,
Gone through the phases of life,
A hand that has tried to soothe pain,
A loving hand,
A tired hand,
A quick hand,
A gesturing hand,
The hand of someone who has been through much.

The hand of a daughter,
The hand of a wife,
The hand of a lover,
Of a mother, of a writer,
Of a photographer, a poet,
And yet do I really know this hand?

Beyond the Borders

*L*osing oneself,
Can this ever happen,
"How can we lose ourselves?" one asks.

Lose yourself in a piece of poetry,
In history, philosophy and psychology books,
Lose yourself in music,
The cadence, rhythm, beat and pulse,
In a world of make-believe, feelings and stories.

Lose yourself in a walk on the beach,
In the crashing, cresting waves,
In a rich world of sea creatures,
Carrying on mysterious lives.

Lose yourself in a star-studded sky,
In a galaxy, a milky way,
An infinite, unexplored world
Beyond our imagination,
When the world around you is for once,
Silent, asleep.

Lose your spirit by diving to an unprecedented depth,
The depth of religion,
Spiritual ecstasy,
Renewal,
Rejuvenation.

Lose yourself by connecting to the One,
Connecting to the Prophets and Angels,
Connecting to the essence of humanity,
Bridging the path
Between the world of the living and the everlasting.

The Need

The little girl romped, raced, reveled,
Living in her little wondrous world,
Surrounded by loved ones,
The familiar,
Comfortable,
Her satisfaction boundless,
Her happiness intact,
Her dreams fulfilled,
Reflecting the lavishness, fruitfulness of her evergreen
garden.

On a stormy day she headed to the garden fence,
Seeking shelter,
The little slit in the fence drew her eyes,
Peeking at her neighbor's garden
Glimpsing a fascinating world,
Where butterflies, bees, deer frolicked,
Where the sun shone bright,
Sparkling water fountains gushed forth,
Water lilies, daisies, orchids bloomed,
Outshining her golden, purple, red flowers.

The little girl turned back to her garden,
Shaking her head,
Dissatisfied with the sight,
Wanting, desiring the other,
Beyond her reach, beyond her reach, beyond her reach.......

The Unseen Universe

Surrounded by the crowds,
Talk, chatter, activity,
Yet alone, insulated.
Putting up a front,
Joining in, mingling,
Mind elsewhere,
A world apart.

The fantasy of a parallel universe:
A truth felt and lived by her,
Its dimensions clear,
Its mesmerizing allure
Filling her every waking moment,
Thronged with memories,
Blinding colors and visions,
Filling the emptiness,
Of the expanding, invisible
World of her own.

Connections

"You are an old soul" she said
Looking at me eye to eye,
"You are wise with a beautiful soul," said another.

My heart unfurled, skipping a beat,
My eyes turned inward seeking the depth,
My hands slowed down, quick gestures for once quiet,
As time slowed down for us,
The connection overwhelming.

As they opened up their hearts,
Sharing their innermost selves,
In the midnight hours,
Revealing the pains and joys,
That shaped their paths,
Honoring me with trust,
With the start of real friendship.

Days and months passed,
The words and looks lingered,
Refusing to fade.
How can they in these days,
Days of the material,
Days of plenty,
Days of quick hellos, quicker good byes,
Share so much,
Link so quickly, find a soul mate?

As the ship of life carries us,
On an uncharted journey to the unknown.

The Dance

*I*n the quiet,
      stillness,
            darkness.

When every breath is a loud shout
      sentences peek out,
            images flourish,
                dreams bloom.

Open buds awaiting,
      blessed rain drops.

Thunder booms
      crashing,
            twisting.

The mental zaps of energy
      set the music in motion.

An invisible maestro leads
      the thunderous orchestra,

Of dancing thoughts, images
      joining in the waltz of inspiration.

The Unfurling

𝓟eeking out,
Shyly striding into the light of day,
A sliver of radiant hope
Finally dares to step out.

The emotional tides
Sweeping her inner core,
Bombarding her relentlessly,
Till the stifling walls in her harden,
Harden, harden, harden and crack,
Ominously.

Emerging a woman strong,
Proud,
Confident,
Unafraid of her limitations,
Wise beyond her years,
Taming the tides,
Gracefully and skillfully,
Strong and ready
To take on the coming storms of life.

The sliver fans out,
Spreads into a radiant shining Circle of Light.

Contours

My Joy

The joy she gave me,
When she arrived,
Kicking, yelling, blue in the face
So tiny, with perfect little hands,
So helpless, flaying about.

The pleasure she gave me,
With her first kiss, first hug, first goodbye,
The wonder of finding her tiny shoes on the doorstep,
The pleasure of rubbing against her silky cheeks,
Of patting her dry after a warm-scented bath.

The happiness she gave me,
From her very existence,
My baby, my first born, my delight!

II

The young girl sits quietly for once,
Contemplating the future,
Expectations, dreams, hopes abound,
She gazes up looking from her computer,
For once still, silent.

Oh how the years have passed,
Her very stillness, momentary stillness
Reflects her growing, maturity, deep thoughts.

My young girl is sitting on the brink between two worlds
Of childhood and adulthood,

Looking back with longing at the years past,
Looking forward with anticipation to the coming years.

My 'joy' is still kicking and on the go,
A tomboy in eternal jeans,
Talking and joking a mile a minute,
Staying up late in the company of Buffy and Angel,
Yet her sharp intellect continues to expand,
As new horizons summon with all their allure.

I pray to the One to keep her safe,
To aid her in her present and future,
To reach her potential and live her dreams.

The Gentle Heart

I look at my son's face,
His is the visage of our ancestors,
His is the face of my father,
That wonderful gentleness,
That kind soul,
That learned mind,
That eye for beauty,
And above all that great heart,
Embracing the family
Me, my son, and our ancestors
In love and tenderness.

My Father

*H*e sits at his desk
Day after day,
Year after year,
Turning away interviews and work.
"But I have work," he says.
"I have work to keep me busy for years on end,
I work for the Lord."

He writes on history and religion,
On the Prophet and his life,
He writes
Not for fame,
Not for a name.

Shoulders bent,
Eyes staring into the computer screen,
Hands flying over the keyboard,
Books opened and closed,
Littering the desk and the room,
He continues his self-imposed mission,
Long into the night.

Grandma

She was a forgiving woman,
The most forgiving I've known.
Wrongs, slights, anger,
All pardoned by that most generous soul.

She was knowledgeable,
Knowledgeable about human ways.
Not with knowledge gained from books,
But from her inner soul.

Faith, healing, loving were her essence,
For family, friends and people from afar,
Sitting peacefully with a gentle smile
In her Hijazi dress
With its white shirt and silver buttons,
Scented with *anbar*,
Bringing up generations,
Generations who will remember her,
Her essence to be followed,
Her story,
Taught and told.

Sitti

She has gone,
Vanished in an instant,
In a traumatic moment,
Time slowed down for those left behind
Shock,
Disbelief,
Grief,
Left in her wake.

That gentle soul,
That slow tender smile,
That age-weathered visage,
That cheery heart-felt laugh,
Quickly quietened with her hand.

The passing of a heart full of forgiveness,
Full of faith in the One,
Leaving behind a legacy,
Attempting and failing,
Living up to an ideal,
My grandmother, *Sitti* Aminah.

*Sitti is the Arabic title for grandmother

The Leave-Taking

I sat close to her shrouded body
Reading the Holy Book,
As her soul departed for the Heavens.

We,
Those left behind,
Sitting together yet apart,
Remembering,
Remembering her gentle, forgiving soul,
Besieged by memories,
Of her smile
Of her hearty laugh,
Memories of her scent and dress.

Alone,
With my own recollections,
Of her soft cheeks,
Of the humorous twinkle in her eyes
Her playful teasing at games with grandchildren
Her quick and steady hand,
Stitching delicate patterns,
Onto the white cloth of homemade pants
Sewn with love for a beloved family.

Everyone,
In his and her own cocoon,
Yet as the day wore on,
Her body was laid to rest.
We turned to each other
For solace.

Contours

We were one, in our shared grief,
Strengthening our ties in this unforgettable time.

Her passing,
Her leave taking,
Unbidden,
Unexpected,
Unannounced.

We bid her farewell,
Yet she remains ever present,
In our memories, dreams and souls.

Adored Essence

The Arabian jasmine's soft petals call out,
Sitti's voice echoes through,
The years trip past,
To the past.

Silvery braids brushing her waist,
Soft coils swinging in the breeze,
Crowned with the white stars of *full*,
Glittering in the early morning light,
Scooping the beloved blooms into water bowls,
Threading them into strings, rings, necklaces.

I reach up, running my hand,
Through the shining strands,
Brushing the flower coronet across her smooth temple
Lean in,
Sniffing,
Imbibing,
Anbar and *full*,
Filling my lungs with her unique fragrance.

Smiling, she hands me her necklaces,
Feather-light touch on my tiny neck,
As the petals settle across my shoulders,
Embraced by her scent with every move.

Every bush I pass revives Sitti's essence,
The call of her favorite bud,
Eternal.

* *Full* is Arabian Jasmine

The Streets of Makkah

The streets of Makkah,
Long bordered with tall, tall homes,
White-washed homes, wooden homes,
Built on every corner, mountain top, ridge,
On the valley floor of the sacred land.

Tall, tall homes,
Centuries old homes,
Studded with brown aged latticed windows,
Overlooking mysterious labyrinths, winding walkways,
Alleys echoing with the passage of sounds,
Voices of those long gone.

Voices of families, friends all known to one another,
Welcoming strangers from other lands,
Spending *sheeshah*-filled nights,
Quiet nights, loud nights,
In the open on the *dakkah*,
Hours of tea drinking, hours of tales,
Brimming with told and untold stories,
Of past generations, present generations,
Held in the collective memory,
A memory retaining the glorious past,
Undeterred by the present.

* *Sheeshah* a water pipe used by men and women
** *Dakkah* a raised bench

Gone are the Days

Of walking the safe streets,
Nodding to every passer-by,
Of streets shadowed with flickering lantern lights,
Filled with throngs of simple, kind folk,
Sellers' cries ringing out, announcing wares,
Boys running through the crowds,
At ease on their own,
Enjoying the nightlife.

Gone are the days
Of simple pleasures,
Reading bedtime stories,
Sleeping on the roof with unpolluted breezes,
Swaying the bedding, caressing the innocent and old.

Gone are the days
Of simple tasks,
Braiding a daughter's hair,
Hugging a grown-up son,
Bringing a surge of fulfillment, of delight.

Gone are the days of fun family gatherings,
Families there in times of happiness and need,
Gone are the days when friends were there for life,
Sharing one's life to the fullest.

Gone are the days of warm-hearted neighbors,
Taking care of one another,
Coming to the aid of the sick,
Of knowing each family, every child on the block.

Gone are the days and nights of old Arabia.

Savored Moments

She skipped down the staircase,
Barely watching well-worn steps,
Taking the curves, nooks in the sides
Quickly,
Dizzyingly,
As the lantern light shed its glow
Within the multi-storied Makkan home,
Lighting the winding path,
Joining the dispersed household.
Her heart contracted, soared,
Eyes glowed,
Trembling with excitement,
To see her father.

A last skip and she is there
Knocking softly,
Her young palms sweaty,
The hard wooden door shut tight,
She pushed the panel and there,
Steadied herself,
There he was.

Surrounded by his students,
The lucky ones from distant lands,
Holding them in thrall,
Sharing his waking moments, meals, knowledge,
Sharing his life,
Family and others rarely seen.

She keeps her head down,
Peeking at the imposing figure,

The Unfurling

Her throat working,
Head rising proudly,
Her gaze roving,
Hungrily taking him in.

Her thoughts settle,
Hugging and hoarding the sight,
Storing his dear presence in the pages of memory,
His calm face, wise eyes, broad shoulders,
The love she feels surges through her,
Warmth coats her heart,
Tears held back,
She savors him with all her might.

Will his gentle eyes favor her with a smile,
Will he crook his finger,
Hold out a warm hand,
Seat her next to him on the right
As she settles in
To briefly share the scholar's world?

Strokes of Tranquility

*H*ard, care-worn hands,
Lovingly gliding on the coffee pot's sides.
He hunches over the pot,
Shining the copper and buffing it,
Humming to the refrain of the swishing cloth.

Catching sight of the feet,
Gently, he lays his beloved bundle aside,
Dusting off his hand he greets the visitors:
"Come in, *marhaba*,
Come in, *ahlan wa sahlan*."

Showing off his treasures,
His children from places far flung,
Rugs, enamel, silver work, saddlebags, glass lanterns,
The progeny of his wise choices.

Serving hot, minted tea,
Soothingly slowing down the hectic rhythm of visitors,
The very act of slowly sipping, sipping, sipping,
Bringing on contentment.
The pace of the past brought back mercifully,
Fleetingly.

Love for his work is evident,
Carrying on in the footsteps of his forefathers,
His life one of survival.

The Unfurling

He keeps his sense of pride, his modesty,
"My children are educated, working in offices,
But this is my lot.
Al hamdu lillah, thanks be to God."
Eyes content, spirit at ease.

As we leave he picks up the coffee pot,
His reflection there clear and direct,
Unwavering,
For all to see.

Arabian Nights

*W*hen the call of the *hudhud*,
Echoes through the palm fronds
Carrying in their mists,
Visions, memories:

Caravans of high spirited steeds,
Crisscrossing the endless seas of sand,
Rushing through the oasis,
Free, yet under control.

Of women washing in the hot springs,
Sheltered in the evergreen palms,
Weaving baskets,
Cooking, sewing, scampering after the herds,
Of days filled with toil.

Visions, memories:
Cascading starlight,
Casting its mild light over campsites,
The moonlight's silver shadow
Illuminating bearded faces,
Young boys thumping their feet
To the wild desert drum beat,
'*Dana, ya dan dan*'
Singing of the pearls in the far away gulf.
'*Dana, ya dan dan*'

The Unfurling

The warm cardamom scented breeze
Carrying the fresh coffee aroma,
Warming, sizzling in the golden hooked pots
To the young giggling girls
Shyly peeking from behind the partitioned tent wall.
Flames flickering in the pit
Wood slowly consumed, sparks flying,
Dancing to the strain: *'dana, ya dan dan.'*

The cry of the *hudhud*
Sweeps through the quiet morning air,
To the dawn of a new century.

Visions, memories,
Blown away by the winds of change.

* *Hudhud* is a bird known as the hoopoe.
** *Dana* refers to a type of Gulf pearls, and the refrain
'dana ya dan dan' is a popular one used in Gulf songs.

The Lure

Treading along, trudging on
The tides of golden sands
Glistening, glittering,
Under the merciless sun,
Giving space and taking space,
As I enter the forbidding, desolate terrain.

Steps slowing down,
Gazing at the golden dry rivers,
Turning dark brown at night,
Their luster dimmed with the dimming of day,
Hiding, enveloping thousands of creatures,
Stealthy, silent, cautious wonders of creations,
Invisible to the eye,
Trailing tiny tracks tracing the ground
A testimony to the existence of life,
Silent life.

II

In the deep, deep darkness,
Stillness filtering in,
To a stillness of the very being.

The light of a thousand stars the only glitter,
Sisters to the full-fledged moon,
Ruling the sky
With majesty.

The Unfurling

Patient palm trees endlessly standing,
Standing alive and standing dead,
Another inhabitant in a world of survivors.

The harshness of heat, the harshness of life,
The dryness, aridness
At bay in the nascent night,
As the breezes pick up
Carrying the music of the *'ud,*
Soft whispers carrying across the dancing dunes,
Campfire light flickering red hot,
Cracking and crackling,
Harbinger of warmth,
Heralding hospitality,
Harkening us with images of the days of yore.

Miles of tides, tides of sand
Moving through time and distance,
Dunes traveling the desert,
Slowly, silently shifting,
Joining an endless line.

Traversing the fierce terrain of life.

* *'Ud* is a type of mandolin.

The Imam

*H*is shoulders straight,
Tread confident,
White upon white,
White trimmed beard, white thobe, white prayer beads,
Purity personified.

He heads out to the mosque,
Smiling his gentle smile,
Gazing with scholarly eyes at the world,
Greeting young and old,
Along the sidewalk,
Embracing the familiar in the courtyard,
Spirit high, entering the peaceful hallowed hall,
Heading to the bookshelves,
Running his hands through the Book,
Pages touched, turned, read and pondered over
By thousands, tens of thousands,
He kneels, reads, and is content.

The prayer call rings out,
He heads through the forming columns
Of black and white,
Of visages from distant lands.

The Unfurling

Bonded at this special time,
He heads for his place,
People part,
He heads them all.

With his vast learning,
Wisdom and forgiving soul,
His melodious voice praises the One
While all join in harmony,
Seeking forgiveness, peace and blessing.

Imam is the Arabic word for leader

Call to Prayer

*F*riday, the rush is on,
"Come on, come on, get ready,"
My son begins the scramble.
Into the bathtub for the usual cleansing,
He lingers on and on.
Knocking at the door,
I end up shouting "Out, out, please."

Steam-filled bath is finally abandoned.
Slicking down his black locks,
Spraying cologne,
Pulling on white pants, white thobe, cuff links, watch,
"Come on, you will be late, get moving."
"Okay, *okay* mom."
He rushes to the waiting car, to a patient father,
His shoes half on, half off,
And I sigh.

Pick up my Qur'an and settle down to peace.

Silent Screams

The unending blows fall,
Enduring the pain is a challenge,
A way of asserting his dignity,
Of standing up for himself,
Pride intact,
Internal screams filling his young mind,
A deluge of tears withheld,
Shuddering,
Shaking.

Dignity held onto tightly, tightly, tightly
Afraid to let go and shatter
Afraid to scream, and never ever stop.
Ever, ever stop, stop, stop.
The word is there on the tip of his tongue:
Stop, oh pleeease.

He continues to outlast the tight fists
As each blow reverberates, resonates
Throughout the very foundations of his tiny frame,
Suspended between the conscious and the unconscious,
As his cowed mother looks on with vacant eyes
Watching wretchedly,
Wondering when.....
When will it will end,
Silently praying,
As both wait for the end.

A last shudder shatters the sibilant silence.

Nocturnal Visitations

*V*isitors of the night
Pass through our souls, our spirits
Lingering,
Evolving,
Connecting those living with the living,
Connecting those living with those long gone,
Carrying hidden messages
For those who can glimpse their fleeting forms,
Foretelling the future, foraging through the past.

Heralding visions of pleasure, visions of horror,
Arriving uninvited naturally,
Arriving uninvited forcefully,
Will these frequent familiar guests,
These nightly arrivals,
Ever cease their call,
Clamoring for attention,
Clamoring for reason, for logic, for interpretation?

Will their fleeting traces be always felt,
By those with an eye for the beyond?

Memories

*P*rayer beads in hand,
Slowly rotating, revolving, rippling,
Wearing the smooth stone in her veined hands
Soft skin, soft stone, soft heart.

Hours, days, months, years
Pass,
Memories
Revisited,
Of old mud-brick homes,
Lavish, sturdy lambs wool cushions,
Straw rushes,
Open windows and doors,
Welcoming light and night,
Copper coffee pots atop firewood,
Children playing under the swaying palms,
Boys dancing with sticks,
Girls braiding hair,
Mothers cooking,
Fathers conferring,
Sumptuous meals laid out for the crowds.
Weddings, feasts, births and deaths.

Memories ebb, flow, align and scatter
Children grown, gone
Giggling grandchildren visiting,
Bringing sunshiny laughter
New homes,

The Unfurling

Comfortable sofas, Persian rugs, closed gilded doors,
Electric kettles, radios, television sets,
Silver coffee pots on marble tops,
Quiet days, hectic days, treasured days
What is left?

She gazes at the soft stones, the soft hands.
Soft gaze, soft heart fills with memories,
Soft lips stretching wide in remembrance.

The Darkness

When the walls close in,
When emotions buffet,
The simple moments,
Of laughter, love, friendship,
Will light the path.

The veil of darkness will dissolve,
Making way for hope everlasting.

The Road Taken

The valley of life,
Invites us to explore,
The valley of life,
With its twists, turns,
Its highest peaks, hollows
Draws one on the journey.

Living the stages, layers, phases
Evolving, changing, growing,
Taking on the thrills and dilemmas,
Each leaving its mark,
Shaping pieces of the puzzle,
Shaping life.

As we live several lives,
Each a different stage,
A stage with its goals, dreams, frustrations,
Touched throughout by the lives of others,
Joining us all,
Binding all in a circle of ever-changing lives.

The valley, will it be long and winding,
Will it be rugged and cut short?
Can our essence, spirit,
Leave a bit, a glimmer
In the hearts,
The memories of those left behind,
Those navigating,
The valley of life?

Equilibrium

As the world I know changes, alters, transforms,
Caught between two worlds,
The clamoring of each tugging at one,
Each pulling in a different direction,
The mind and heart at war.

Buffeted by the demands of opposites,
Balancing on a tight tangled wire,
Teetering as I look down at my feet,
Carefully placing each foot,
Weaving, wavering, peeking down at the looming abyss.

Puzzled,
Intrigued,
Enticed,
Excited,
As people take up the banner
For a way of life,
For a way of thought,
Each puts forth arguments, logic, merits,
Espousing and advocating
New thoughts, entrenched thoughts,
Different outlooks, familiar outlooks.
I adjust internally, adjust externally,
The two worlds affecting the depth of my core.

Will the two worlds finally converge,
Or will they tear the fabric of my identity,
Bringing forth a rebirth?

The Calling

The Muse has departed,
Bowed down,
Fettered in chains,
Abolished,
Logic flown before it,
Integrity turned into itself,
Truth shed off its mantle,
Sanity throws in the towel.

Vulnerable writers, powerless poets,
Cry out for freedom,
As daunting, global tirades
Name opposing voices traitors and cowards.

What is left for them,
The writers and poets?
But the Mighty Pen,
Instrument of quiet power,
Instrument of dispelling untruths,
Instrument of Light in the Darkness.

The Mighty Pen
Will serve its purpose, imprint its mark,
Bring forth the light of hope
Bring forth a measure of balance,
Ringing in logic, justice, freedom and sanity.

The Muse is back to stay.
Singing its Siren's song forevermore.

Crossroads

From Womb to Tomb

*F*rom womb to tomb,
An entire nation
Is condemned.

From womb to tomb,
The oppressed cry for an end.

An end to massacres, beatings and tyranny,
An end to repression and humiliation,
An end to the murder of young and old,
The shooting to kill or maim,
The burning of olive groves,
The destruction of homes,
The enslavement of a nation.

All cry out:
"When will it end?"
From womb to tomb it continues on, and on, and on……..

The Bleakest Night

This piece was composed following the first in a series of bombings in Riyadh, Saudi Arabia, on May 12, 2003 in which 30 people were killed.

The blackest, bleakest night descended
On the land of praying palm trees.

The guardian kingdom,
Lies open and bare.

With its shattered peace, shattered innocence
In the wake of rancorous explosions.

Fair is foul, and foul is fair,
The world lies on its hinges,
Askew.

Right is wrong, and wrong is right,
The wicked work of blinded messengers of death,
Rocked the nation,
Roiled nations.

Dark deed done in the darkness of night
Under the hate-laden hovering cloud
Of fanaticism, utter ruthlessness,
Of hatred for the Other.

Future generations
Will bear the stigma,
Of weapons used to vanquish the unarmed.

Of innocent people from all creeds,
Lives torn asunder,
A blemish shared by all.

No oceans will cleanse the stain
Remembered with loathing by all.

II

The blackest, bleakest night,
Soaked with the blood of the innocents.

As demented, lethal minds,
Planned and went about their unholy work.

Cloaking their viperish, venomous deed,
In the name of a peaceful religion.

Carrying out the mission of death,
Death of Muslim-mandated tolerance,
Death of historic ties with the People of the Book.
Death of illustrious Islamic honor,
Death of long-held values,
Death of the essence of their faith.

Attempting to shake the very name,
The venerated spirit of 'Salam,'of peace.

The peaceful in 'Islam'
Ripped out of the word,
Ripped out of their merciful faith.

Crossroads

A molten lava of bitterness,
Spewing forth resentment,
Sowing the seeds of anarchy.

Fanaticism rearing its ugly head,
Brazenly flouting the very principals Islam espouses,
Of equality in the eyes of the One.

Dealing the death blow to their pious calling,
Exposing their warped thinking to the world.

Their people, their land refute them,
Consigning them and their arcane act to the devil.

Will the bleakest night ever be forgotten?

The Decree

The judge wields the gavel
Pounding it on the scarred table
Craaaack,
The sound landing hard
On our sensitized hearing.

We hold our breath,
Terrible silence descends.

The prosecution rests,
We wait restlessly,
The verdict is pronounced
The hush thickens.

Every Muslim, Jew, Christian,
Black, Indian, Chicano,
Guilty, guilty, guilty
For daring to exist,
For straining to survive.

Cheers ring out
As the lynching mob moves in
Giddily slapping their comrades' backs,
Amassing atop the mountains of ashes
Jostling over their clean, easy kill.

As bowed, chained tolerance is led away
Sucking in its tumultuous passing
Assassinated freedom,
Brotherhood,

Crossroads

Unity of faiths,
Unity of people.

A void looms, dotted with the remainder
Of their scattered ashes.

Our fear rises,
Waves of despair threatening to drown us.

Seeking an escape from the inescapable
Choking and gagging,
We head out the door,
Gulping, gasping,
Breathe in the stench of ashes.

Will the tides of change bring forth a rebirth?

The Ambush

*H*e watched the old movie unfold,
The headcovered man bashing his van into a building,
Nodding his head: 'Yes another one, they are terrorists,'
The calm way he uttered those words
The look in his young eyes,
Made me ache.

For they had won,
Hands down they had won,
Ultimately they had won,
Their hollow victory turning the world upon itself.

Those demented fanatics have implanted the bitter seeds,
Our young believing that terror is here to stay,
Questioning their identity constantly,
Questioning elements of society, a fact
Could I really answer?
Did I even *want* to answer?
No justification, no excuse can wipe,
Needless deaths, destruction of innocents,
Not a single life lost could be justified.

The land turned into a big gated occupied territory
The once-peaceful kingdom rent with shootouts,
As the tolerance of our spiritual beliefs
Is hijacked, twisted, used.

Power-hungry zealots
Misguided by the need for vengeance,

Crossroads

Vengeance against perceived,
Unacceptable ways of life,
Those whose hearts have been wiped clean,
Clean of the basic tolerance for fellow man,
A tolerance making the religion thrive,
A spirit attracting billions to the faith,
All dashed on the rocks
In the surging ravaging river of loathing the other.

As the very essence of our faith now stands in danger
Of this ambush from within,
Turning back upon them,
Derailing their intentions
As hate colors their vision of the truth,
That we are all, all, all
Sons and daughters of Adam
That the three faiths,
Our mainstay, our guide
Are interlinked, bonded forever
Sealed by The One
To spread their message of peace for human kind.

May 2004

The Shackled Slumberers

The voices of nations
Silenced.
Generations upon generations,
Stifled.
Powerful, creative minds
Seized.

Thoughts, dreams, aspirations
— God's gifts to man —
Aborted.
When will they be able to grow,
To live,
To thrive
In the expanding universe of possibilities?

Will the nations manacled by a few,
Consigned to an etherized death-like slumber
Break the shackles that bind?

Will the people awaken?
Will their craving the ideal,
Will their cry for freedom
Be heard?

The masses are stirring,
Setting forth for that worthy quest,
Will they find holy freedom's grail?

The Awakening

A dove watched from its perch
As streets turned into seething fury,
Tender children lost,
Lives taken before their time,
Mothers shell-shocked,
Unshed tears shimmering in their eyes,
Fathers wounded both in heart and soul,
Carrying the young bodies,
Wrapped in white cloth,
Taken to an everlasting life.

Tears of anguish and rage,
Streamed in rivers across the lands,
As young and old watched in disbelief and fury.

Raging crowds stirred,
From Cairo to Jakarta,
From the Persian Gulf to the Atlantic,
In answer to the call of departed souls, broken homes,
Widowed wives and homeless millions.

Images flashed across screens of the globe:
Of flights of the homeless,
Living off the land in tented cities for years on end,
Of earlier unforgettable massacres,
Images of bloody mutilated bodies swept beneath bulldozers
As Deir Yasin, Sabra, Shatila and Qana are unburied.

The Unfurling

"What can we do?" cried youngsters in Egypt,
In Istanbul, London, Washington,
"I will take up the banner, I will fight, fight to the end,"
Cried Ahmad al-Shafi,
Leaving his home in Egypt, running off to Palestine,
"I will not stand still," cried the 12-year-old boy.

The fight is not over,
The long sleep that shackled generations is over.
We will rise once again.

Generations upon generations will take up the fight,
"Carry this message to the heavens,
Carry this message to our children,
Carry it to the world."

Whispered the souls of the dying to the dove.

The Return

The five lay side by side,
Their tattered books,
Their belongings strewn across their bodies.

But that couldn't be, shouldn't be, mustn't be,
The world asked,
"Can such a thing happen?
In this civilized world of ours?"

The five,
On their way to school,
Joining millions around the world,
Happily swinging their bags.
The five,
Their small shoes shined,
Their uniforms straight and neat,
Happy to meet their teachers and friends,
The sound of their laughter carrying across the lane,
Silenced forever.

The five,
Greeted by the Chariot of Death,
Following an earlier, more thunderous greeting,
Of the deafening booby traps,

Leaving in their wake,
Mothers, souls wrenched asunder,
Fathers with much-loved memories,
Of musical laughter,
Of mischievous innocence.

The Unfurling

The five,
They returned,
Not to their families' loving arms,
But to their Creator.

High in the Heavens,
He embraced them in His benevolence
Accepted them back into His care.

They returned,
Not to the uncaring, cruel, blind world,
The world of the raging beasts,
The world of the savage soldiers,
The world of the Palestinian downtrodden.

This poem was written in memoriam of the five children aged six, 10, 12 and 14, of the Al-Astal family from the Khan Younis refugee camp who were killed by the Israeli military in November, 2001.

Over 30,000 mourners attended the funeral and a call was made for an international investigation committee to look into the murder of children and to determine Israel's responsibility.

The Unanswered

The elephant thunders and charges,
Stampeding the helpless hordes,
Disrupting the order of the disordered,
As old and care-worn women, men and children,
Shiver and take flight.

Fleeing their havens and hearths
In despair,
As the rest of the uncaring world
Goes about its business.

Countless thousands are on the move,
Wandering and questioning the hardened world,
Seeking a mirage, a sanctuary.

With shell-shocked visages,
Tear tracks running down smudged cheeks,
A proud people,
Brought down low.

Once more on the move,
With tattered clothes, empty hearts and bellies,
Beseeching,
With unanswered questions.

Will the unending years of war end?
When will the world let them
Till and build,
Learn and grow,
When will it let them live?

The Unfurling

Or is it not their lot,
Is it not the lot of Afghans to live in dignity?
Is it not their lot to walk across their lands
Without exploding land mines under their feet,
Maiming millions young and old,
Without the roar of lethal planes filling their skies,
Day and night,
Mowing and mauling life indiscriminately,
Setting off cries of helplessness, rage and vengeance?
In Kabul, Kandahar and Kunduz,
From barren terrains to rugged mountaintops.

Is it not their blessing,
To appease the hunger of their families,
To seek unbombed hospitals,
To pray in houses of worship unharmed,
To eke an honest living and sleep,
The sleep of the world?

Nightmare

The bleak, owl-omened cloud thunders,
Pealing woes, worries, rage and rancor,
As the 'mighty' unleash their ferocity
At the helpless.

Another once-mighty nation
Tastes the bitter dust,
Standing on the edge of obscurity,
Where once,
The majestic ruled
In a golden era
Of discovery, learning and science.

Where the cradle of civilization
Birthed generations
Of achievers, builders, scholars,
Poets, writers and calligraphers.

The forgotten tread of thousands
Echo in the hallowed halls
Of universities.
Remnants of museums and mosques
Stand sentinel,
Silent and bare.

The city dwellers, marsh people and villagers
Groping under the cover of darkness,
Looking for lost family and friends,
Eking out a living,
No one can begin to conceive.

The Unfurling

All is laid to waste
As Baghdad, Basra and Mosul
Are assaulted yet again,
In the name of 'good.'

Forgotten:
The richness of the past,
The milk of human kindness.
Bomber jets sweep the skies,
Raining their fatal bounties.

Laughter, hope and dreams
Of generations to come,
Banished behind an iron wall.

Will they ever show their countenance
To the people of the ancient land?

Recipe for Knowledge

*O*pen up canned books,
Fork out the subjects,
Spread out the math, science, history, literature,
Slather with flowery phrases,
Mix in tongue-twisting passages,
Spice up with lengthy, peppery pages,
Heat, simmer till dried into a solid mass
Of intimidating, mysterious tomes
Cool, and turn on their sides,
Brush with the yolk of white wishy-washy learning.

Measure in years of memorizing,
Pick over each word carefully,
Dice up creativity into slim, slim slivers,
Sift and wipe clean of creativity,
Prune and slash threatening questions,
Beat in harshness, discipline,
Mix it well; mix it well.

Add mandated narrow dogmas,
Sift out other approaches,
Skewer systematic planning,
Wash away the roots of ingenuity,
Scoop out criticism,
Stuff the tender shoots, receptive brains
With reams of evaporated needless figures and facts,
Freeze for decades.

Bring out and dust off any residual powder,
Defrost the books, systems and schools,

The Unfurling

Sprinkle in new frustrated teachers,
Sift in tiny, tiny specks of training,
Spread on rich, thick layers of low budgets,
Mix with needy, demanding parents,
Drain out their questions and comments,
Set students aside for later handling.

Bring to a boil,
Run through numerous studies,
Offer tiny sips to well-formed committees,
Remove after years of contention.

Set on a new shiny silver tray,
Rearrange the mixture into new patterns,
Turn into delicate, aromatic appetizers,
To appease the hungry nation.

Feed them till every didactic morsel is devoured.

Voices

In memoriam of reporters harassed, beaten and killed during "Operation Iraqi Freedom." Over 13 journalists were killed during the war, and the bombardment of a base of unembeded foreign media outlet at a hotel in Baghdad touched many across the globe. Composed in April 2003.

The crowds gather,
Mourning the death,
The leave-taking burdens souls and hearts,
As advocates of telling the story as is
Are targeted, an example to the rest,
Conventions, values and principles flouted.

Truth terminated,
In the service of such worthy causes,
Its essence eroded, confined and now tethered,
In the name of "freedom," of "democracy."

Can we lament the dawn of a new era,
As petty minds rule,
As the voices of truth
Are targeted, muffled and silenced?

Freedom of speech,
Freedom of thought,
Freedom of expression,
Lie buried in a wasteland,
Beneath mounting piles of rhetoric.

An iron curtain of secrecy and oppression descends.

The Muse

How it carries us through,
Taking on a life of its own.
Putting pen to paper,
Moving one beyond the world,
A doorway onto other dimensions.

Yet is stronger still as words, images tumble,
Written in the dead of night,
In the darkening hours with little light,
Light's light? Or is it illuminating light?

The Spell

The crashing waves,
Gently receding, marking the sand,
Whispering,
Chanting a music of their own
For those who lend a listening ear.
Can we lend them our ears?

Gazing into cresting waves,
Attempting to capture their soundless songs,
Looking across majestic peaks,
The silence of the land echoes within me,
Finds a resonance that will remain forever more.

A memory that will haunt and beckon,
To this mystic land,
The land of turbaned people,
Bewitching travelers through the centuries.

I am not alone in my net,
Hooked and not wanting to wiggle free.
Thousands of feet have trod this land,
Merchants, sailors, adventures, writers
All have tasted its enchanted air,
Wanted to linger and become part of the fabric,
Of a gentle people, generous people
Of the people of Oman.

All have gazed across the ever-changing sea,
The cresting waves,
And remembered the serenity of the peaceful land.

The Gait of Courage

*W*alking down Washington Street,
Bothered by the humid air,
Tired, out of sorts.

Carrying heavy bags of books,
Thinking of the distance yet to go,
Long strides slowing down,
Frustrated at the slowness,
Need to get back, fast.

A glimpse of a man walking in front
Stops me in my tracks,
Heart swells with pity,
Dread and pity.

Awkward, unbalanced gaits,
Twisted knees, arms waving,
Yet on, and on he walks,
Slowly, but persistently,
Grey haired and gentle looking,
Determined to make it back home.
He walks up the curve,
I slow down, watching him, thinking.

Oh, the courage,
A car comes zooming in, ready to swerve and hit him,
His arms wave at the driver, stopping him in his tracks.
A woman looking on freezing up,
Both of us let out our pent up breath,
Smiling our eyes connect,
I slow down again, watching.

He passes young girls in halter tops,
Young men in long jockey jerseys shouting at each other,
Musicians, businessmen, shoppers, policemen,
He passes them all, and keeps on.
Surrounded by the busy street,
Busy life,
Busy onlookers,
Few pay attention.

Pity turns to admiration,
To awe,
My gait picks up,
Yet now, even the slow gait is accepted.

Boston August 13, 2003

The Court

In a world of heat,
A world of creation reigns.

The master glass maker
Rules a kingdom of fire, water, air.
Turning molten fluid
Into life,
Lovingly, skillfully,
Jewel-hued splendor emerges.

Gifts drawing us onto the journey,
Of fragile and hard, hard and fragile.

In the world of the master glass maker.

Santa Fe July 31, 2003

The Coming

The young shoots spring forth,
Seeking sunshine, care and love.
Will they be able to grow,
Will our world take the new generation
With all its hopes,
Aspirations,
Dreams,
Concerns,
And nurture the tender shoots?

Will they be understood,
Their talents appreciated,
Their ambitions fulfilled,
Their creativity given free reign,
Their free spirits valued?

Or will they be controlled,
Belittled,
Derided,
Cut down,
Ignored,
To lie withered,
Unable to grow and bloom.

The choice is ours,
The custodians of the newcomers.

The Meeting

Meetings can be planned,
Can be expected, looked forward to.
Meetings can come about suddenly,
Yet the best is the meeting of the like,
Of the mind.

But can such a meeting be understood?
These genuine bonds
Enrich and expand,
Touch our lives
In untold ways,
Ripple across the ebb and flow of daily lives.

Meeting of the minds,
A wonder to behold,
A well of giving,
Of joining.

The Serenade

Time and distance widen the gap,
Rivers of inner sorrow buffet the heart,
Slamming and fluttering,
Strong beat echoes through the body,
Thumping a sad serenade.

A body intact on the outside,
Bleeding and scarred on the inside,
Layers of hurt,
Layers of sorrow,
Unending, unrelenting,
Forming, building up, unraveling.

Layers are exposed and peeled away,
The shedding of the layers
Agonizing, slow,
Exposing the inner being,
The frailty of life,
All pared away,
Slice by painful slice,
By the knife of time.

The Loss

They say you get over the pounding pain,
That it will slowly fade,
The scars will heal with time.
Can they truly ever understand?
The gut-wrenching agony,
The daily in and out,
Throbbing,
Constant ache?

As memories assail of lost ones,
How can they imagine the suffering will ever fade,
Ever, ever, *ever* fade?

Places and homes they had trodden,
Words and phrases they uttered,
Little expressions, small facial gestures,
Joys and sorrows they shared,
Habits, foods, routines,
Clothes they loved,
Their very smell,
Presence,
Essence,
Vanished forever.

How can it be dealt with
In silence?

In the inner soul and depth of the heart.
Deep and deeper in the heart,

Crossroads

A damaged heart that keeps on, on, on
Beating,
Thumping,
As if life is fine,
Regardless.

Lost Love

She knelt in the soft warm sand,
Her long black hair shimmering in the warm breeze,
Black hollowed eyes shadowed and dim,
Holding in their depth an indescribable pain
Shoulders hunched protectively,
Softly she brushed the dearly held box,
Trembling hands caressing the carvings,
Bidding it adieu.

Cradling it as she digs a hole,
A hole to bury the treasure
Deep and deeper yet,
For she has lived for years with her beloved burden,
And the time had come
To let it go and go on,
She buried her pain,
Her sorrows and unfulfilled dreams,
Deep and deeper yet.

The treasure of lost love,
Left in the sands of time.

Yearnings

*Y*oung love sweeps in,
Charging in,
Taking hold,
Taking control,
Giddiness, happiness, sorrows magnified.

Wanting to be in each other's company every moment
To share every little happening,
Each experience, thought,
Hours of talking, yearning,
Hours of sadness,
Days of sorrow as the bond unravels,
A treasured memory in the album of life.

Mature love gently sweeps in,
Excitement is there, held in check,
The needs are there,
Slower, gentler to form,
Joy builds up,
Appreciation,
Sacrifice,
Giving,
Forgiving,
Lessons of life color it all.

The Script

*L*ost in the crackling pages,
Captured,
Enriched.

Curiosity satiated for a time,
Time forgotten in the rush.

A rush, a thirst, a search
Enfolded in a world of the unknown.

A world of curves,
Beguiling scripts,
Conquering the imagination,
Dazzling the heart,
Letters, words, sentences,
Capturing the spirit of the scribe.

Wringing out new thoughts,
Ringing in fresh realizations, knowledge,
Thoughts swirl and coalesce,
Form a new nexus.

Years pass,
Pages turn,
Obeying the call,
The call of a questing mind,
Craving of a searching heart.
Replete at last,
Or still pining for the yolk of wisdom?

The Relentless Visage

She is always hungry for more.
Her hunger unabated,
Needing, seeking and thriving,
In times of war, distress, sorrow,
Grief.

Will she continue seeping into life
Rendering one helpless,
Or will she be able to shed her mantle,
Pick up the threads of existence,
And continue the daily toil?

Expectations

The burden is heavy
Growing heavier yet.
As time passes by,
More is added on, added on, added on……….

No one can envision the burden,
Invisibly lugged on the shoulders,
Felt with ever-increasing awareness.

The weight of expectations,
Unsaid, unarticulated,
Yet there for the long haul,
In the past, in the present.

Baying for attention,
Responsibilities, duties, expectations,
Competing with wishes, dreams and needs
Pulling one in half,
Growing cumbersome,
Piled on through the years,
Heavy, invisible shackles.
How can they be borne,
With welcoming spirit or with a need for escape?

Power's Glory

The siren's call
Beckoning, beguiling,
Powerful,
Intriguing.

Can one resist it,
The siren's call?

The limelight,
True and false adulation,
Earned and unearned respect
Turn one's head.

Can fame and fortune,
Can being in the glaring spotlight
Make one swim, dive and ride on
In a sea of contentment?

Or will one drown
In a sea of sorrows
Once the legend fades,
Or will one drown
As expectations fall apart,
Will the siren's call ring as true?

The Choice

"*D*on't worry, let it go."
"Don't worry, it doesn't matter."
Those words softly spoken,
Oh, the harm they can do,
Belittling feelings,
Of the inexperienced, the naïve, the innocent.

"Don't worry, it will pass."
Bringing perspective to bear
To the more experienced,
The mature,
The hardened.

Is the world worth this much agony?
Are the trouble, sleepless nights, worry,
Worth it in the larger scheme of life?

What will happen, will happen,
Fate, life will continue,
Striding regardless,
Along their unwavering path.

In the Wake of the 11th

Our people are distraught,
The blanket of peace ripped aside,
Exposing us to the vagaries of the unknown.

Long cocooned in a world of plenty,
Long used to the net of safety, easy life, friendly people,
The new upheaval shocks all.

An awakening to a nightmare of uncertainty,
A new life, a new path.
Will we be able to weather the coming cataclysm?

Banishment

I release you my beautiful, terrible fear
                        -Joy Harjo

I let you out,
Your rule is at an end,
I let you out,
With all that is in me,
Grief,
I let you go,
Pent up wrath,
Clawing at my heart,
Clenching my hands,
Running your despairing, devastating course,
Through throbbing veins.

I give you back
To the oppressors,
Tyrants,
Soulless,
Callous of human decency,
Giddy with hysterical racism,
Puffed with blind arrogance,
Thriving on their mastery,
Stealing, raping, conquering,
The Arab world, African continent, Asian lands.

I let you out,
As the agony of generations
Birthed,
Matured,
Ingrown,

Stamp our collective memory,
Moaning mothers,
Massacred young innocents,
Shamed helpless males,
Weaved in and out of the centuries.

I turn you out,
Grief,
Out of my heart of hearts
Out of my soulful soul.
I let you out,
As women's tears join
Across lands, deserts, oceans
Rivers of suffering,
Gushing and flooding,
The tributaries of time and place.

I let you go, Grief,
So you can no longer hold me in thrall,
Keep me from restful sleep,
Smothering my dreams,
With a bleak, murky future for my loved ones.

II

I let you out,
Grief,
And pick up the mantle of joy,
Pulling its swirling warmth tightly,
Deeply drinking up bubbling pleasure,
Dancing and twirling
To the ecstatic, mighty music of human bonding,
Soothing,

The Unfurling

Supporting,
Succoring me,
Bringing me peace, peace, peace, peace…

Oh, yes, Grief, listen well,
As the bloom of hope thrives,
Spreads its fine pollen,
Cultivating laughter,
Confidence to take you on.

As streaming, quickening hope enters my soul,
Courses through my blood,
Races through my heart,
Shines out of my eyes,
I let you go,
Shrieking, writhing in denial.

Trying and failing,
To survive in a barren land,
Banished from the light of day,
Banished from the soothing dark of night.

Your rule at an end.

Eclipse Reversed

The bombardment booms
    Thundering
        Crashing
            Zipping and zapping through the core.

Sustained blows ferociously fall
    As brutal words bombard the ear,
        Tearing,
            Shredding,
                Clawing,
                    Rampaging.
As scars refuse to mend
    Felt deeply,
        Darkly,
            Devastatingly.
An open incurable wound
        Leaving a lingering residue.

How long can hurt be sustained
        Hours, days, years?

II

As the protective layers form,
    Shaping up,
        Coalescing,
            Banding up,
                Building up bit by slow bit,
                    As the inner self arises.

The Unfurling

From a need for preservation,
    Of self,
        Of sanity,
            Preservation of life itself.

Daily sorrow winding its way
        Through the core,
            In and out, in and out.

Layers merge,
    As the light of life peeks through,
    As daily blessings are noted,
      Graces and thanks,
        For the bounties of the Merciful
                Surface.

Short Pieces and Haiku

*I*t all comes easily from the heart
       supporting, sympathizing, empathizing

Sweeping across countless lives
       swift sands flittering across endless dunes

Will the grains of giving
       be treasured, hoarded polished pearls

Or will the grains dissipate
       till nothing is left of oneself?

Restoration

Minds clouded, confused
red rage reigns
the world tips, will it revive?

Tide

The whirlwind
      sweeps in frenzied minds
              ruled by intolerance.

Cataclysm

Mindless puppets, mindless leaders
   The world suffocates
Innocence and peace massacred,
   Under the yoke of ego and retribution.

The Summoning

*W*hispers clamor
    Deserts call out
        For the lost ones' tread.

Revelation

*I*solated, harsh desert
        Cracking, moaning fissures
Opening onto the world
        Can exposure be that painful?

Facets of Farewell

His smile belied his last sleep
Family surrounded the shroud
Farewells till the next meeting.

Pure of heart, pure of soul
Lightly carried
On the upright shoulders of mourners.

Buried with a baby
Could he have wished
More innocent company?

The light body picked up
Speedily, laying him to rest
His sons gazed on in a haze.

The Tug

Cherished bonds,
  tie the soul, pull and plummet
    glorying in their power they climax.

Exuberance

Lyrics pound,
  mind and heart rejoice,
    humming the song of life.

About the Poet

Nimah Ismail Nawwab is a Saudi poet descended from a long line of Makkan scholars. An English writer, editor and poet as well as photographer; her essays and articles on Saudi society, customs, Islam, art, crafts, cuisine and calligraphy have been published in Saudi Arabia and abroad.

Through the years she has also given presentations on Arabia, wedding customs, Ramadan and women in Saudi Arabia, 'Women in Islam,' in Washington D.C and in Holland on "The Role of Saudi Women in the Media."

Writing poetry is another unexpected and exciting venture that began in 2000. Her poems on women, freedom, Arabian society, the younger generation of Saudis as well as the universal themes of love, loss and the simple joys of life have been widely excerpted online and in print. A few poems have been translated into Arabic and some of her poems have been used by educators in Saudi Arabia and abroad in their English literature curriculum and at poetry workshops.

Nimah's involvement with poetry has resulted in readings for students, teachers and general audiences in Saudi Arabia. Her immersion in the arts has led to new ventures including the production of a music and poetry CD based on poems featured in this volume.

Nimah's interests include photography with an emphasis on portraits, weddings and nature shots in addition to studio photography and developing. She is interested in the layout and design of print and websites.

She collects Saudi artifacts, Middle Eastern folkloric costumes, silver jewelry, Persian rugs, Nomadic weavings and pottery. She loves animals and enjoys listening to eclectic music, especially when writing poems; traveling, cooking and researching international dishes.

Nimah lives with her husband and children, Aminah and Ibrahim, in Dhahran, Saudi Arabia. She welcomes comments and feedback from readers and may be directly contacted at Nimah@TheUnfurling.com.

Selwa Press was originally established in 1999 to publish English language books concerning the early history of the Kingdom of Saudi Arabia. Today the Kingdom's history is being rewritten on a daily basis, so we have widened our scope to include significant works about present day Arabia.

In Arabic, selwa *means comfort or solace. It is our intention to continue publishing books that offer* selwa *to the hearts of our readers everywhere.*

Additional copies of Nimah Nawwab's **The Unfurling** are available directly from Selwa Press via internet, mail or phone.

Online, go to www.Outintheblue.com and click on the icon for **The Unfurling.**

Mail customers may order by sending a check or money order to:

> **The Unfurling**
> Selwa Press
> P.O. Box 3650,
> Vista, CA 92085
> Or call toll free at 866 AT SELWA (866 237-3592)

The cost per copy is $14.95 plus $5 for Priority Post shipping within the USA.